T0113548

Words That Create Wellness:
Using Affirmations And Afformations

Words That Create Wellness:
Using Affirmations And Afformations

Dr. Robert L. Wilson Jr., DSL

Archway Publishing books may be ordered through booksellers or by contacting:

Archway Publishing
1663 Liberty Drive
Bloomington, IN 47403
www.archwaypublishing.com
844-669-3957

ISBN: 978-1-6657-3671-8 (sc)
ISBN: 978-1-6657-3672-5 (e)

Library of Congress Control Number: 2023900536

Print information available on the last page.

Archway Publishing rev. date: 02/10/2023

Contents

Acknowledgment

I would like to acknowledge and thank my lovely wife Tamika, and my four beautiful daughters Jewel, Jasmine, Joy, and Jillian for the great lesson that we learned about the power of using our words with the rice experiment that we did.

Wellness is not merely about achieving good health. It's about the choices you make in the process of creating how you want to exist and live. Wellness is a journey, not a destination. The journey is within yourself, discovering, unlocking, and maximizing your awareness of the real you.

In *Words That Create Wellness*, author Dr. Robert L. Wilson Jr. shows you a new way to think and speak about wellness. This conversation and dialogue is about how powerful your words are, and it's through affirming and afforming spoken words that you release that power. This provides more understanding of how to intentionally incorporate your words into the practice of creating wellness.

Words That Create Wellness empowers, educates, engages, and encourages you to create and live your life now. Wellness is created through the words, inner dialogue, and statements you consistently and continuously speak about you and your life. Learn how to use your words to work for you instead of against you.

Introduction

This book's purpose is to raise awareness, build literacy, and increase wellness from the inside out. The psychology of wellness takes into consideration the inner nature that is essential to guiding and governing our lives in a fruitful, productive, and effective way (Arloski 2014).

An integral function of education is building literacy. This book will focus on doing just that through self-education in the forms of self-awareness, self-determination, and self-talk to help you create wellness. *Self-education* means both awareness and knowledge of who you are, how you are motivated, what your determination levels are, and what your abilities are to speak information that will cause transformation in your daily practices in a meaningful way. Self-education is about aligning your self-identity, your belief system, your capabilities, your behaviors, and your environment for your desired wellness.

Use this guide to help you on your journey toward maximizing your potential. You'll be able to fulfill your purpose and increase your success—starting from the inside out! First you should read and reflect on the information in each section and answer the questions; then apply the information into your strategic plan for each dimension of wellness at the back of the book.

Wellness is about the choices you make in your process of creating how you want to exist and live, not merely achieving good health. Wellness is a journey, not a destination. The journey is within yourself, finding an awareness of the *real* you—the awesomely wonderful being you were created to be. A big part of this journey is awakening to discover who you are in order to unlock your capabilities and maximize your possibilities for success. Welcome to the journey of a lifetime!

I developed this book in order to provide a new way to think and speak about wellness. This conversation is about how powerful our words are, and it's through affirming spoken words that we release that power. This provides more understanding of how to intentionally incorporate your words into the practice of creating wellness. Words can be used strategically to program your desired image of wellness, reflective of the eight dimensions of the wellness model that works to provide the process for the programming and belief system. That switch is on default, and the behaviors and practices are habitually followed.

Your words can produce the life you want or the life you do not want. It's yours to choose, so choose wisely. What you speak, you become. You are limited by your casual speech (Gomas 2017). Discover the power of your words and how to use them to intentionally describe, in detail, how you want to live. Use your words to unlock the power you possess to play with the possibilities and create opportunities and outcomes for your good. Maximize your results by strategically identifying specific words that paint the visual, auditory, and kinesthetic sensory perspectives needed for creation. In other words, you will see, hear, and feel—first internally and then externally. Everything is created twice—first on the inside; then on the outside. After I realized that everything is created twice, I knew that finding wellness was within reach if we could just understand the words we speak and how to use them to intentionally create what we want.

This book is meant to be started at the beginning and gone through to the end in order for you to understand the concepts, digest the content, and apply it to your life using inspired action to get results. Read and reread it, because it will help you shift and reshape your beliefs, perceptions, thinking, and—more importantly, your words—to create.

Words

The words you use can create the life you want or the life you don't want. The words you choose to speak and think are what will reinforce your life. Either way, you'll get what you say you will. Your words are containers that carry out the power of your thoughts and the pictures of the life you do or do not want that determine your life's results; therefore, we should be very intentional with the words we choose to use. Words create images, feelings, and emotions, and the more we hear certain words, the more embedded the images, feelings, and emotions become for us. Words provide a detailed vision for the life you want to create (Arloski 2014).

Say words with feeling and hear them with your emotions to create the self-image that will program your behavior. Hearing words with your emotions means that you attach emotions to the words and the pictures or images that have been created. We will not just be using any words; the words we will use are called *affirmations* or positive, present tense affirming statements and *afformations* which is asking yourself a question or series of questions in a positive way to engage your thinking from the place of answering from the inside what you desire and want. It is using your inner computer to help you search for answers to the question or questions you have programmed yourself to search for. By learning about affirmations and afformations, you will gain an understanding of how to use your words intentionally and strategically to be empowered to create the life you want—first internally and then externally. Your words have power!

Your words create your power and release it into action. Genevieve Behrend, author of *Your Invisible Power*, states, "In your every word there is the power germ that expands and projects itself in the direction your word indicates, and ultimately develops into physical expression" (Behrend 2013). The purpose of the following exercises in this book are to guide you in the learning process, self-discovery, shifting your mind, and taking inspired action using your words to intentionally change your results.

Want … Become

Words take you from what you want to be to what you become. Words help you decide and describe in detail what you want or—in some circumstances and situations—what you do not want. Words help you to clarify and identify what you desire. Using your words in the present tense through conditioning will take you from what you want to becoming your desire.

Want starts the process, but what you become fulfills it. It's important to use affirmations to pinpoint what your desires for wellness are. You must constantly speak your affirmations and afformations with a positive emotional attachment in order to help you feel and become your desired self—something that's necessary to create the outcomes and results you seek. You will go through the stages of acknowledging your current state, to knowing you want something to shift, to transforming to become what you want to be. We will discuss writing and defining affirmations and afformations later in the book.

Study and Practice

"The only way to develop understanding is through study" (Proctor 2021). Awareness should lead to studies that give you a greater understanding of how to apply content that can transform your life practices. The self-education component that's needed for true change to take place is not in studying information for information's sake, but instead in studying yourself and how the information specifically raises your awareness, increases your understanding, and effectively demonstrates practices that foster and create greater wellness results and outcomes for you.

You must develop the habit of repeating this information in the words you say in order to expand your thinking and belief systems to support the new wellness images you are creating within the eight dimensions you desire (Proctor 2021). By studying this material, you are learning, unlearning, and relearning how to build your self-image and connect your feelings and positive emotions as you program and reprogram the paradigm using words that will produce the behaviors and the external results you want.

By creating affirmations that build good feelings and foster positive emotions, you will enhance the power of your self-talk and will be able to create and support the eight dimensions of wellness results you desire. This leads us into discussing the role of self-talk in your wellness journey.

Self-Talk

Self-talk is an important aspect of your self-image. Many use negative self-talk to reinforce their inner critics instead of their inner cheerleaders; however, I would like to discuss healthy, positive, intentional self-talk to create the self-image of wellness you desire, which you can do with the words you choose to use. Self-talk is important in both internal and external communication for producing results and outcomes.

Self-talk can be heard internally and externally. Your speech should be aligned from the inside out. The words you speak within yourself should consistently match the words you say out loud when describing your image and desired outcomes. The first step in creating positive self-talk is to notice your self-image and which words you use to create and reinforce that image. You must recognize the power that lies within you and your words. Your words embody your thoughts and the very essence of your creativity and, when used intentionally and with feeling and consistency, will create the circumstances, conditions, states, and wellness you desire (Behrend 2013).

Your self-talk is what creates the narrative of your inner thought process, which is constructed inwardly and projected outwardly. Understanding the function and operation of your inner talk can empower you to strategically and intentionally use it to build your desires and wellness. Your outer world must agree with your inner conversation. Your inner speech reflects how you feel inside, for the inside mirrors the outside (Murphy 2010).

So what are you saying on the inside?

Self-Talk Exercise

Take fifteen minutes to write down and reflect on whatever self-talk or inner dialogue happens within you. Is it more positive or negative? This chatter is happening, regardless of whether you're aware of it. I want you to become aware and mindful of the inner communication patterns that exist within you. Before your words will change outwardly, they must change inwardly. Silence your inner negative voice because what you hear and speak will become your reality (Gomas 2017).

Self-Image and Words

What is self-image? Self-image is the view you have of yourself. It is constructed internally based on your thoughts, experiences, and the words you use or that are used toward you. Your self-image influences how you see yourself and what wellness looks, feels, and sounds like to you. How do you create your self-image?

Affirmations and afformations use words to create pictures that become powerful containers to carry your thoughts into the image you have of yourself. Your words help create the images and feelings you have about yourself, planting or programming the self-image internally, which is then reflected externally. The emphasis is on the importance of creating your self-image and connecting it with your words. Affirmations and afformations work together to create this image that determines your wellness. Deeper work on self-image takes awareness in order to explore internal and external barriers that have been governed by our words (Arloski 2014).

Words are maps of your internal reality and external results. They are the doorway to the internal workings of a person. It's important to find out what's behind them. What is the meaning of your words? How do your words describe your world? Your words help determine your level and degree of wellness. Words create wellness. The words you speak help create the wellness or lack of wellness you experience.

Your words carry the power of the image. You release that power by declaring words consistently and with deep feeling. You must intentionally take control by releasing the power of what you want by speaking affirmations and afformations based on your personal wellness goals. For example, I speak affirmations and afformations daily and listen to them on a recording to start and end my day. Listening repeatedly to my affirmations and afformations when I first get up, throughout the day, and at the end of my day helps to recalibrate and reconnect my mind to the images, feelings, and emotions of my desired wellness.

Self-Awareness and Self-Determination

It's important to raise your awareness of how your words can work either for or against you. Your determination and motivation will work in conjunction with your awareness of how to apply the appropriate information into action with your words.

Self-awareness is your ability to recognize the words you intentionally use to reflect various aspects of the eight dimensions that contribute to your wellness. Self-awareness is consciously noticing the words you use concerning the outcomes and results you get.

Self-determination is your ability to intentionally and consciously use your will to focus and change the aspects, components, or factors that contribute to your wellness choices. Your wellness behaviors are reflective of your level of self-awareness and self-determination connected to your self-image. Self-determination is intentionally using your words to create what you want.

Self-Determination Theory

It's important to recognize how affirmations and afformations influence your motivation. You must take responsibility for your life and circumstances in order to be truly empowered (Gomas 2017). One of the first areas you should take responsibility for in your life is your mouth by choosing the words you use when speaking to yourself and others. There are a few things you should consider when discussing motivation. The self-determination theory captures the essence of motivation.

The self-determination theory was implemented in this book to assist with the self-education of motivation. This will help you become aware of *how* you are motivated, which impacts your level of determination to accomplish your wellness goals. Many try without truly understanding how determination and motivation work. It's beneficial to recognize both the challenges and opportunities that will increase both motivation and determination individually. Having self-awareness will give you ways to increase your motivation and determination internally and externally, which can positively impact your outcomes and results.

The self-determination theory focuses on competence, relatedness, and autonomy as the main ingredients that will help you to understand your ability to create your desired wellness based on the level of determination to make the changes for that outcome (Martela and Ryan 2015). A major element of the self-determination theory is the self-education of internal and external motivational factors. Motivation will help you set goals for and reach positive outcomes with support through autonomy, competence, and relatedness (Ryan and Deci 2020).

People become more confident when they improve their skills and become more competent. Confidence comes from competence. Your identity and beliefs must be aligned with your capability to demonstrate the necessary behaviors to create outcomes that reflect your self-image. Your ability to connect related meanings increases your motivation and determination to accomplish your goals. The concept of autonomy—or the freedom to choose what one wants and how one wants to do it—inspires many to work toward completing their goals.

What are your motivations?

Internal – things that motivate you from within yourself

External – things that motivate you from outside of yourself

Transfer of Learning Theory

Being aware of how you learn and of how to transfer what you've learned in this book into your life practice will gird your determination to achieve your desired wellness and success. An important part of having knowledge is transferring what you've learned into practice. In this section we will discuss the transfer of learning theory. This theory is based on the concept that knowledge learned in one area can be applicable in and across multiple contexts, settings, scenarios, and situations. This theory is helpful with guiding the self-education process because this information ensures you can apply or transfer the acquired knowledge from this book in various ways and under different circumstances (Hajian 2019).

The transfer of learning is so important because a big part of defining your self-talk for wellness comes through studying and discovering yourself. That study of discovery transfers into what you're learning, as the only way to gain knowledge of yourself, self-talk, wellness, motivation, and the creative process is through study and by intelligently organizing and directing the knowledge into practice (Proctor 2021).

Not all knowledge, however, is transferred into effective learning. Some habits that help the effectiveness of transferred learning are: reflection, application, skill enhancement, and self-education (Hajian 2019). All these elements are included in this book to assist with the transfer of learning what you read into your actual practices hereafter.

Let's discuss the importance of the transfer of learning theory and the self-determination theory in this process.

Transfer of Learning Theory and Self-Determination Theory

The transfer of learning and self-determination theories provide a great set of tools to help you gain awareness of what influences your motivation, determination, and self-education. This allows you to better understand how to best put into action strategies and practices for your success. Knowledge itself is not power, but the power of knowledge is knowing what to study and how to apply it for yourself (Proctor 2021). That knowledge and learning should include intentionally raising awareness, building literacy, and increasing wellness from the inside out. That leads us into discussing the roles of study and practice in the transfer of learning on your wellness journey.

Wellness

Wellness is about using a dimensional perspective to gain a more holistic view of your life choices and understanding how that process can work for your good or your bad. You choose. Maybe a better statement would be that you have already chosen, whether consciously or unconsciously.

I wanted people to have an easy read full of vital information to allow them to see new facets of themselves—to extract and draw out the values people already have in them, like creativity, resourcefulness, and wholeness (Arloski 2014). This insight helps build resilience and purposely improves your confidence and competence to create optimal well-being. Here are the tools; you just need to know how to access and use them.

Wellness impacts and affects overall quality of life. Many people begin their journeys of wellness in response to illnesses. I want to allow you to gain new awareness and shift your perceptions to take into consideration developing optimal wellness. Pursuing optimal wellness is a choice to improve without limits predetermined by other situations or circumstances. The goal is to discuss wellness in this capacity to empower, educate, and enlighten you to recognize the importance of intentionally improving your wellness by building resilience and raising your awareness, understanding, application, and encouraging your best practices for seeking optimal wellness in a personal way.

Eight Dimensions of Wellness Model

- Spiritual—feelings of fulfillment, purpose, meaning, and identity that aren't necessarily based on any specific religion
- Intellectual—using your mental and cognitive capabilities to create, expand, and think in healthy ways
- Emotional—awareness, recognition, and ability to shift feelings
- Financial—literacy, awareness, and freedom regarding money matters
- Physical—exercise/activity, health, nutrition
- Social—healthy, happy, fulfilling relationships and interactions with others
- Occupational—finding fulfillment and purpose in work that increases skills, satisfaction, and empowerment
- Environmental—creating physical and mental settings that are conducive to feeling safe, supported, and stimulated

For additional information, use this link for the SAMHSA website: https://store.samhsa.gov/product/What-You-Need-to-Know-About-National-Wellness-Week/sma16-4952.

These definitions are provided as a baseline for you to explore, study, and more narrowly define what they look, feel, and sound like for your wellness.

The eight dimensions of the wellness model will help you take into consideration other components and aspects of life that impact your overall well-being. This model will also help you identify different areas of your life in which you want to improve wellness. Although this book focuses on the eight dimensions of wellness and talks about wellness dimensionally, it is more of a holistic approach to recognize how each dimension of wellness feeds or funnels into the overall wellness we experience.

Eight Dimensions of Wellness

(Define each dimension in your own words)

1. Spiritual

2. Intellectual

3. Emotional

4. Financial

5. Physical

6. Social

7. Occupational

8. Environmental

Words and Beliefs

We have already analyzed how words connect to your self-image and wellness, so in this section we'll go deeper to learn about affirmations and afformations. In this book, we want to raise your awareness to help your use your words to create a new identity and set of beliefs in the eight dimensions of wellness. The words we use to create beliefs are called *affirmations* and *afformations*. Your words are containers of creative power and force that take the pictures or images you create and intertwine them with your belief system. What words are you using? Are your current beliefs serving you?

Now we'll discuss what affirmations and afformations are. Your words become a powerful indicator of your beliefs and your results. Your words carry the power of what you believe and will create it within your very own life. It is important to use that power to create the exact life you want.

The power of your life is in your words (Proctor 2021). The power is in consistently speaking the words that create the life you want. The method of repeating words in the form of affirmations and or positive questions in the form of afformations makes your desires and wellness limitless because the words you use to describe, define, and create your world are determined by you (Behrend 2013).

Affirmations

Affirmations, or intentional words, are spoken to positively influence your reality. What are you saying about yourself and your wellness?

Here we will learn what affirmations are and how we can intentionally use them. Affirmations are powerful, positive, present-tense statements for empowerment, and they build your mindset and belief system to embrace the new or desired perspective. Affirmations mixed with an emotional connection to them will create images and paradigms, and they will program or reprogram the way you think.

Affirmations are more than confessions of something you sort-of desire or "That would be nice" statements; rather, they are statements of power and direction to feed your self-image, create feelings, and program behaviors toward wellness goals and plans. You are encouraged to embrace time for the development of powerful, positive, present-tense statements to help you capture the level of wellness you desire (Arloski 2014).

Words create pictures and images that are related to the pictures and images we see externally. A creative way to program your self-image is to say out loud that your desired result has already occurred. This mentally switches your imagination to work for you to create the feelings and behaviors associated with the desired goal.

Negative Affirmations

This section of the book discusses negative affirmations. I want to demonstrate that nearly everyone already uses affirmations—just not positively. Negative affirmations create negative images, pictures, feelings, and emotions. In many situations, negative affirmations create self-sabotaging behaviors and language. This is a way to program your self-image by verbalizing out loud undesired results from places of past disappointments, hurts, or failures, which mentally switches your imagination into working against you. This produces self-imposed limitations, frustrations, and a stuck state of being.

Negative affirmations might sound or feel like:

- Things are always happening to me.
- Nothing is working out.
- I'm broke, sick, unlucky, tired, unhappy, alone, unsuccessful, etc.

- I can't get a break.
- It's too late for me.
- There's nothing I can do.
- I'm always in this situation.
- I don't belong.

These are just some examples of negative affirmations. If negative affirmations are contributing to how you feel, then ask yourself, *How is this serving me?* What are your current outcomes? Is this your desired goal? You have the power and ability to change your affirmations, which will change your language, self-image, and results.

Afformations

An affirmation tells your mind what you want, and an afformation allows your mind to reinforce what you want. Afformations are powerful statements or ways of asking yourself questions with a positive spin to utilize your brain capacity and mental functions and faculties to search for ways to support the question you are asking yourself. They are powerful, present-tense questions for empowering and developing a mindset and belief system that provide you with insight and strategies into what, why, how, when, and where the new or desired perspective will become your reality.

Afformations allow you to use your mental faculties and capabilities to think about solutions to problems instead of only focusing on the problem. Focusing on the problem only reinforces the problem, not the solution. By strategically asking powerful questions that guide you in gaining new insights, perspectives, or answers, you can shift your wellness images dimensionally to assist changing behaviors and outcomes.

Positive afformations sound and feel more like, *Why am I so successful, so happy, so productive?* This switch programs your mind to start finding reasons to support these statements. Afformations help readers create an image of wellness by talking through questions that add in details and describe the wellness image (Arloski 2014).

A creative way to program your self-image is to verbalize out loud questions from a positive experience that has already occurred. This will mentally switch your mind into working for you. By asking yourself the afformation, or question, of *why* the self-image of wellness you desire exists, you help create and reinforce the feelings and behaviors associated with your desired goal already being fulfilled and achieved, which is needed in wellness creation.

Negative Afformations

Now let's discuss negative afformations. Many people accidentally use afformations against their true desires by allowing their minds to reinforce what they don't want.

Negative afformations are powerful statements or ways of asking questions with a negative spin that misuse your brain capacity by searching for ways to reinforce the negative questions you ask yourself. A negative way to program your self-image is to verbalize questions out loud that would lead to undesired results that come from places of past disappointments, hurts, or failures that have previously occurred, which mentally switches your imagination to work against you to create the feelings and behavior associated with the undesired goal.

Negative afformations create negative images, pictures, feelings, and emotions. In many situations, negative afformations create self-sabotaging behaviors and language similarly to negative affirmations. This produces self-imposed limitations and frustrations, along with a stuck state of being.

Negative afformations might sound or feel like:

- Why are things always happening to me?
- Why am I unsuccessful?
- Why is this not working?
- Why does this work for everyone but me?
- Why is everyone else successful?
- Why do I keep ending up here?

- Why do I feel nothing is working?
- What's wrong with me?
- Why me?
- Why am I not happy?
- Why am I not successful?
- Why am I not rich?
- Why do I feel like if it's not one thing it's another?
- Why don't my relationships work out?
- Why can't I find the right person?
- Why can't I find the right job?
- Why can't I get a break?
- What's the holdup?
- What's wrong?

These are just some examples of negative afformations. If you're using words like these and creating negative feelings, ask yourself, *How is this serving me?*

What are your current outcomes? Do they reflect your desired goals? You have the power and abilities to change your afformations, and doing so will change your language, self-image, and results.

You'll have an opportunity later in this book to write yourself new, positive afformations so you can put what you are learning into practice.

What You Say and How You Say It

When creating affirmations and afformations *what* you say and *how* you say it are equally important. Words matter! Tones matter! Saying things with feeling matters! It's just as important to create positive statements as it is to speak consistently. It's also critical that you say it with a degree of positive emotions in order to reinforce feelings and create the vibrations and frequency that support the self-image you desire and are creating.

What you say creates the image you want, and how you say it creates the feelings or vibrations that accompany the image. This produces the internal desire, and if you consistently speak it, it will start the internal process that will outwardly manifest your desired results.

Conditioning

Words work by conditioning your mind. Just like someone exercising and working out their muscles, your words work out your results and outcomes. The more you intentionally and strategically use your words—affirmations and afformations—you will change your results and outcomes. Affirmations and afformations provide practice and opportunities for your words to condition you internally to externally manifest behaviors and results. Words create vibrations that change the frequency or channel you're putting out. They are creating the result you are getting and what you're attracting. Words carry pictures within us. Your power lies within you or the words, affirmations, or afformations that you speak consistently, emotionally, and intentionally.

Being a spiritual being means you speak thoughts and things into existence. You cultivate your image and work from the inside out. You use several mental faculties, along with your words in the form of affirmations and afformations, to take thoughts or pictures and change them into external things. Your imagination helps build a life you want in detail.

Intuition helps you operate from the spiritual realm of creation by connecting to your infinite source. The Will helps you to hold onto the image you are creating. Reasoning helps you see and play with the possibilities and opportunities available to you as you shift your perception to change how you see your life manifested through images. Words allow you to cultivate your imagination, intuition, will, reasoning, and perception to see, believe, access, and breathe life into what you want from the inside out.

Most people try to change by gaining more information or changing their behaviors. Changing your filter changes your information. It's not the world outside that you should focus on changing, but the world inside of you. Once you change the world on the inside, the world on the outside reflects those changes.

This change is more about internal communication than external communication that is usually the primary focal point for many people. They focus on the words they are speaking out, but it's just as important to focus on the words you're hearing within yourself to declare, decree, release, and to create your world of wellness.

Writing Affirmations and Afformations

Affirmations and afformations should be positive because they can work negatively and in opposition to your true desires and goals. "Positive words generate positive energy" (Gomas 2017). They should be in present tense to assist you with visualizing and feeling the desired goals or outcomes as accomplished, which is important in programming your behavior to connect to the self-image of wellness you are focused on.

Affirmations and afformations should be consistently spoken to program and reprogram your self-image. Visualizing and using your imagination are integral parts of this process. Hearing the affirmations and afformations consistently will reinforce the self-image once created. Feeling and attaching positive emotions with the image connects the internal self-image with the programming and guidance of implementing the external behaviors to reproduce the internal image of the new dimension of wellness desired.

I would like to discuss the power of using *I am* statements when creating affirmations. *I am* statements are spiritual principles for creation and manifestation that shift the power of words to becoming whatever follows *I am* to complete the statement.

I am statements work best when integrated with positive emotions that elicit strong positive feelings to reinforce the statement being made. The power of saying, *I am*, lies in the consistency with which you repeat the statements until the feeling takes over and the statement becomes true.

Speaking the affirmations consistently will help rewrite old beliefs shifting the belief system to the new set of beliefs and wellness desires you want. "Replace negative words with positive ones and low impact words with high impact ones" (Gomas 2017). The statements create the desired reality and truth you want to live by creating the thing twice—first inside then outside.

I am statements speak from a positive place and position of completion and creation.

Examples of Positive Affirmations

Spiritual: I am a strong and powerful spiritual being who creates wellness with my words. I feel and see myself as a strong, powerful spiritual being who creates wellness with my words!

Intellectual: I am calm and relaxed, have a peaceful mind and great memory, and I can think my thoughts into successful results. I feel and see myself as calm and relaxed, with a peaceful mind, a great memory, and the capability to think my thoughts into successful results!

Emotional: I am so happy, grateful, energetic, and I feel great. I see myself and feel happy, grateful, energetic, and great!

Financial: I am a multimillionaire with multiple streams of income. Money comes to me very easily, abundantly, and consistently from multiple sources. I feel and see myself as a multimillionaire with multiple streams of income. Money comes to me very easily, abundantly, and consistently from multiple sources!

Physical: I am very fit, firm, toned, lean, healthy, full of energy, and the best version of myself. I feel and see myself as very fit, firm, toned, lean, healthy, full of energy, and the best version of myself!

Social: I am well-loved, connected, and have the best relationships and people who appreciate and celebrate me. I feel and see myself as well-loved, connected, and have the best relationships and people who appreciate and celebrate me!

Occupational: I am thriving and flourishing with purpose, professionalism, and success as I add value to others. I feel and see myself thriving and flourishing with purpose, professionalism, and success, and I add value to others!

Environmental: I am living in a very wealthy, safe, healthy, stable, and pleasant environment where I grow and expand. I feel and see myself living in a very wealthy, safe, healthy, stable, and pleasant environment where I grow and expand!

Examples of Positive Afformations

Spiritual: What makes me such a strong, powerful, spiritual being who creates wellness with my words? What makes me feel and see myself like such a strong powerful spiritual being who creates wellness with my words?

Intellectual: What makes me have a calm, relaxed, and peaceful mind; a great memory; and the capability to think my thoughts into successful results? What makes me feel and see myself as calm, relaxed, and having a peaceful mind, a great memory, and the capability to think my thoughts into successful results?

Emotional: What makes me feel so happy, grateful, energetic, and great? What makes me feel and see myself as happy, grateful, energetic, and great?

Financial: Why am I a multimillionaire with multiple streams of income? Why does money come to me so easily, abundantly, and consistently from multiple sources? What makes me feel and see myself as a multimillionaire with multiple streams of income with money coming to me very easily, abundantly, and consistently from multiple sources?

Physical: What makes me very fit, firm, toned, lean, healthy, full of energy, and the best version of myself? What makes me feel and see myself as very fit, firm, toned, lean, healthy, full of energy, and the best version of myself?

Social: Why am I well-loved and connected, having the best relationships and people who appreciate and celebrate me? What makes me feel and see myself as well-loved and connected, having the best relationships and people who appreciate and celebrate me?

Occupational: What makes me thrive and flourish with purpose, professionalism, and success while adding value to others? What makes me feel and see myself thriving and flourishing with purpose, professionalism, and success while adding value to others?

Environmental: How do I live in a very wealthy, safe, healthy, stable, and pleasant environment where I grow and expand? What makes me feel I live in a very wealthy, safe, healthy, stable, and pleasant environment where I grow and expand?

Mindset vs Mindshift

To learn about mindset, you must become aware of the thoughts and beliefs that are fixed to the self-image in your mind. Your mindset controls your behaviors and the results you get—hence the beauty of mind shift. By identifying the fixed beliefs that no longer serve you and the new self-image that you want to achieve your mind shift will help you to replace and reprogram your behaviors to support the new image and results you want.

Mindset is a fixed way of thinking that controls what you see, hear, and feel internally. Wellness is a result of the mindset and accompanying beliefs that you have about the eight dimensions of wellness that we use in this book. Mindshift is the new focus and results you are creating within those eight dimensions of wellness.

Mindset and mindshift both deal with your beliefs and are confirmed with your words. Mindset deals with past words and beliefs you've already created; whereas, mindshift deals with creating new beliefs through words in the form of affirmations or afformations that you are now programming into your mind as you move forward.

Your words, in the form of affirmations or afformations, can be either positive or negative. These words create your belief system. "Beliefs determine your behavior, not the other way around. A belief is a strongly held opinion about yourself or the world around you. Beliefs often create habitual patterns of thought that continue to play over and over in our hearts and minds" (Gomas 2017).

Your words reflect your mindset or mindshift. Choose your words wisely. You can tell a lot about a person's mindset or when they've made a mindshift based on their conversation. Indicators of a mindset are phrases like: *it has always been, I always, it never,* or *every time.* Indicators of a mindshift are: *I realize, I now see, I now understand,* or *this is a new perspective.*

These are a few indicators to help you become aware of your words, which indicate either a mindset or mindshift.

Changing your Mindset

Now that we've defined and explained both mindset and mindshift, you may ask how to change your current fixed mindset. You must first notice and be aware of what it currently is. Your current mindset is producing the results—or lack thereof—that you create with your thoughts.

A good way to identify your current mindset within the eight dimensions of wellness (spiritual, intellectual, emotional, financial, physical, social, occupational, and environmental) is to go through each dimension and write down what you see currently in each. That will be your mindset. Now write down in each of those eight dimensions what you would like to see, how you would like to feel, and what you would like to hear associated with each of those eight dimensions. This will take you some time to do. The mindshift is your desired outcome.

The mindshift starts with a new desire that's different from the current status quo. The next step is creating affirmations and afformations to describe what you want to see, how you want to feel, and the words you will use to create what you see and what you feel in the new desired outcomes within the eight dimensions of wellness.

Now attach positive emotions and consistently speak the new affirmations and afformations for those eight dimensions. The more you can feel and see those affirmations and afformations being your reality, the more the shift will move from the inside out. Remember, the outside reflects what's on the inside.

Mindset

Take about fifteen minutes to reflect and write down
your thoughts on the state of your current mindset.
Is it more positive or negative?

Mindshift

Take about fifteen minutes to reflect on and write down your thoughts about what mindshifts you want to make in your life for wellness.

Affirmations, Afformations, Feelings, and Emotions

The way you talk about and to yourself do have an impact on how you feel and the emotions that support those feelings. Saying words with feeling and hearing them with your emotions reinforces the self-image or identity that you have, which manifests in the outcomes and results you get. Therefore, we want to intentionally use affirmations and afformations to create positive feelings and emotions around our wellness goals and desires.

Words without feelings and emotions will not have the strength or force to manifest our desired level of wellness. The stronger the feelings and emotions connected to the affirmations and afformations, the more quickly your desired results will come to be. It is especially important when using affirmations and afformations to create feelings and emotions to see your desired outcome now. The feelings and emotions you would have when that desired outcome is accomplished will help you to create the image, feelings, and emotions to support the external manifestation of that image!

Emotional intelligence is a tool that can be incorporated into wellness practices that will help you recognize the role of your emotions in better engaging, empowering, and enriching your experience. Recognizing good and bad feelings concerning your wellness outcomes is very beneficial. You take control of the process by becoming aware of how to intelligently shift your emotional state to create your wellness experience and results. It provides clarity of your emotions, and the perspective, approach, capacity, practices, and behavior of outcomes regarding shifting your feelings to align or realign these things toward what you want. This leads us into a discussion about programming, process, and practice.

Programming, Process, and Practice

In this section, I want to focus on the importance of programming, process, and practice. Words are critical and crucial in programming the self-image as well as in implementing the belief system in the process, which results in the expression of behaviors in the practice. Programming is a result of words, repetition and emotions attached to those words to provide meaning—either positive or negative—to internally program the behaviors in practice that are seen externally. Many people are unaware their words matter.

Words can be used intentionally to program the desired image of wellness. This is reflective of the eight dimensions of the wellness model. The words provide the process for the programming and belief system; that switch is on default in which the behaviors and practice habitually follow. By gaining awareness of how to program, you will learn the process, the behaviors, practices, and outcomes you can strategically and intentionally identify to your desired level of wellness; through the self-image, affirmations, and afformations to govern the process positively in changing the outcomes and results in your favor. Affirmations and afformations strategically and intentionally monitor and use words to promote your desired wellness.

Strategic Plan

A strategic plan is necessary to successfully apply and implement the information and concepts provided in this book to create wellness. There are several elements or components necessary to create a strategic plan. I want you to use the information you have been completing in the exercises to help you create a plan for your wellness goals.

One way to do this is to create SMART goals. SMART is an acronym to help you tailor your goals strategically and intentionally. SMART goals are *specific*, *measurable*, *achievable*, *relevant*, and address a *timeline*. Please use the following strategic plan worksheet to develop a strategic plan to use affirmations and affirmations within the eight dimensions of wellness to create your desired wellness goals and outcomes.

SMART Goals

1. **Specific**: What are you going to say? How are you going to say it?

2. **Measurable**: How often will you say your affirmations and afformations?

3. **Achievable**: Do you have goals you can realistically accomplish?

4. **Relevant**: Do your goals fit what you want? What would you like to create?

5. **Time**: When will this happen for you? How often will this happen? By what specific time will you achieve the results you want?

Affirmations

Use your words to create your affirmations for your desired wellness goals and results within the 8 dimensions. Be very detailed, descriptive, and clearly define what you want!

Eight Dimensions of Wellness

Spiritual

What affirmations would you like to create for the following area of wellness?

What does it look, feel, or sound like for you?

Eight Dimensions of Wellness

Intellectual

What affirmations would you like to create for the following area of wellness?

What does it look, feel, or sound like for you?

Eight Dimensions of Wellness

Emotional

What affirmations would you like to create for the following area of wellness?

What does it look, feel, or sound like for you?

Eight Dimensions of Wellness

Financial

What affirmations would you like to create for the following area of wellness?

What does it look, feel, or sound like for you?

Eight Dimensions of Wellness

Physical

What affirmations would you like to create for the following area of wellness?

What does it look, feel, or sound like for you?

Eight Dimensions of Wellness

Social

What affirmations would you like to create for the following area of wellness?

What does it look, feel, or sound like for you?

Eight Dimensions of Wellness

Occupational

What affirmations would you like to create for the following area of wellness?

What does it look, feel, or sound like for you?

Eight Dimensions of Wellness

Environmental

What affirmations would you like to create for the following area of wellness?

What does it look, feel, or sound like for you?

Afformations

Use your words to create your afformations for your desired wellness goals and results within the 8 dimensions. Be very detailed, descriptive, and clearly define what you want!

Eight Dimensions of Wellness

Spiritual

What afformations would you like to create for the following area of wellness?

What does it look, feel, or sound like for you?

Eight Dimensions of Wellness

Intellectual

What afformations would you like to create for the following area of wellness?

What does it look, feel, or sound like for you?

Eight Dimensions of Wellness

Emotional

What afformations would you like to create for the following area of wellness?

What does it look, feel, or sound like for you?

Eight Dimensions of Wellness

Financial

What afformations would you like to create for the following area of wellness?

What does it look, feel, or sound like for you?

Eight Dimensions of Wellness

Physical

What afformations would you like to create for the following area of wellness?

What does it look, feel, or sound like for you?

Eight Dimensions of Wellness

Social

What afformations would you like to create for the following area of wellness?

What does it look, feel, or sound like for you?

Eight Dimensions of Wellness

Occupational

What afformations would you like to create for the following area of wellness?

What does it look, feel, or sound like for you?

Eight Dimensions of Wellness

Environmental

What afformations would you like to create for the following area of wellness?

What does it look, feel, or sound like for you?

Reflective Journal

1. What have you learned regarding using affirmations and afformations with the eight dimensions of wellness to create your wellness goals?

2. What new awareness or insights do you have?

3. What do you see, feel, or hear because of this new awareness?

4. What is your current mindset? (Notice *what* you think and *how* you think.)

5. What is your mindshift? (Consider *what* you would like to think and *how* you would like to think.)

Progress and Results Tracker

This section is designed to help you track your progress and results over the next 30 days. In addition to implementing your strategic plan and speaking your affirmations and afformations for each of the eight dimensions of wellness, answer the following questions for each day and record your answers over the next 30 days. Notice your new awareness and insights regarding your challenges, opportunities, resources, progress, and results. How will you use this information from your progress and results tracker in creating a strategic action plan for your wellness goals going forward? What will it look, feel, or sound like for you?

    Here are the questions to ask yourself each day for 30 days -What are your challenges? What are your opportunities? What are your resources?

    What progress have you made? What are your results?

Day

    1.

    2.

    3.

    4.

    5.

    6.

Day

7.

8.

9.

10.

11.

12.

13.

14.

15.

16.

17.

18.

19.

20.

21.

Day

22.

23.

24.

25.

26.

27.

28.

29.

30.

Taking Inspired Action

Now that you have completed the 30-day journey what
are your next steps? How will you use the information and
concepts in this book to help you? How will you apply it
and what will be your daily practices moving forward?

Conclusion

Affirmations and afformations can be used intentionally to program the desired image of wellness that reflects the eight dimensions of the wellness model. Consider wellness as something you create instead of something you achieve. Your power to create wellness lies within you and within the words, affirmations, or afformations you speak consistently, emotionally, and intentionally.

By gaining awareness of how to program the process and what behaviors need to be practiced, you can strategically and intentionally identify your desired level of wellness. Through self-image, affirmations, and afformations you will promote your desired wellness results and outcomes. Develop a strategic plan to use affirmations and afformations within the eight dimensions of wellness to successfully create your desired wellness goals and outcomes.

The self-determination theory and transfer of learning theory are tools incorporated in this book to assist readers with understanding their internal and external motivations to gain awareness of their self-motivation to strategically set goals that include how they are motivated. The learning of transfer model assists readers with using the information from this book in multiple ways across the eight dimensions of wellness. Mindset and mindshift are two very important components and changing behaviors, results, and outcomes.

The study of what motivates and enhances your determination will help as you transfer your learning into real results and positive outcomes. Affirmations and afformations can be used as an emotional intelligence tool that can be incorporated into wellness practices.

Discover the power of your words and how to use them intentionally to describe in detail how you want to live. You take control of the process by becoming aware of how to intelligently and intentionally shift your emotional state through the power of your words to create your wellness using SMART goals to enhance your experience and positively produce results. Use your words to create the life you want!

Bibliography

Arloski, M. (2014). Wellness Coaching for Lasting Lifestyle Change: Second Edition. Duluth, MN. Whole Person Associates, Inc.

Behrend, G. (2013). Your Invisible Power. Watchmaker Publishing, Columbia, SC.

Gomas, D.C. (2017). Christian Life Coaching: Bible. Copyright @ Dennis Gomas.

Hajian, S. (2019). Transfer of Learning and Teaching: A Review of Transfer Theories and Effective Instructional Practices. IAFOR Journal of Education. P.93-111. 7(1).

Martela, F. and Ryan, R.M. (2015). The Benefits of Benevolence: Basic Psychological Needs, Beneficence, and the Enhancement of Well-Being. Journal of Personality. P.1-15.

Murphy, J. (2010). Believe in Yourself. Martino Publishing. Mansfield Centre, CT.

Proctor, B. (2021). Change Your Paradigm, change Your Life: Flip That Switch Now! Gildan Media LLC.

Ryan, R.M. & Deci, E. L. (2020). Intrinsic and Extrinsic Motivation From A Self-Determination Theory Perspective: Definitions, Theory, Practices, And Future Directions.

The Center for Self-Determination Theory (CSDT) Website, https://selfdeterminationtheory.org

National Wellness Institute, https://nationalwellness.org

SAMHSA's Wellness Initiative- https://store.samhsa.gov/product/SAMHSA-s-Wellness-Initiative-Wellness-Community-Power-Point-Presentation/sma16-4955

About The Author

Dr. Robert L. Wilson Jr., DSL is an author, entrepreneur, consultant, speaker, coach, and trainer. He holds a doctorate in strategic leadership, a master's in sociology, and a bachelor's in psychology. He is also a Certified Professional Life Coach, Certified Wellness Coach, Certified Life Coach, Certified Mindfulness Practitioner, Certified Neuro-Linguistic Programming Practitioner (NLP), and Certified Hypnotherapist.

Dr. Wilson is the owner and principal consultant of Robert Wilson Consulting and Wilson Global Outreach Solutions, as well as, the founder and lead trainer of Global Solutions Education and Training Academy. He has worked in the field of mental health, leadership, and organizational development for over twenty years. Dr. Wilson also has a rich background in building and facilitating learning action networking communities. His areas of focus are personal, professional, leadership, and organizational education, development, and training. He is a National Trainer and certified Mental Health First Aid Instructor for the adult and youth curriculum.

For additional information about services, products, or programs, please reach out to Dr. Wilson via the following contact information:

Dr. Robert L. Wilson Jr., DSL, CPLC, CWC
Owner and Principal Consultant
Robert Wilson Consulting
Wilson Global Outreach Solutions, LLC
www.WilsonGOS.com
Robert@WilsonGOS.com
Global Solutions Education and Training Academy

https://globalsolutionseducationandtrainingacademy.learnworlds.com

For Additional Book

By

Dr. Robert L. Wilson Jr., DSL

Printed in the United States
by Baker & Taylor Publisher Services